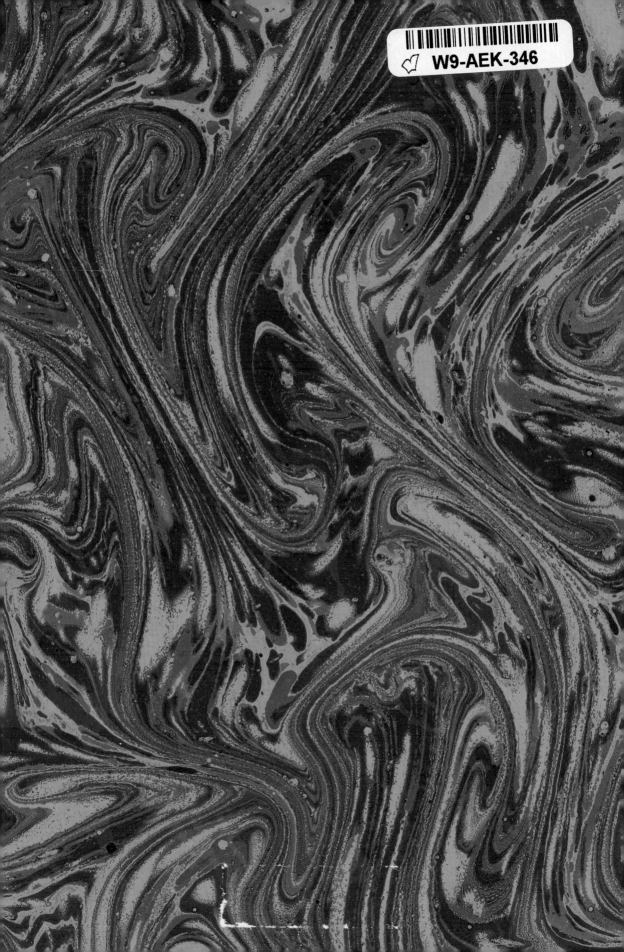

L'ALLEGRO

BY

JOHN MILTON

AND

WILLIAM BLAKE

MIRTH AND HER COMPANIONS

JOHN MILTON

L'ALLEGRO

WITH THE PAINTINGS BY
WILLIAM BLAKE

TOGETHER WITH
A NOTE UPON THE POEMS
BY W. P. TRENT

NEW YORK
THE LIMITED EDITIONS CLUB
1954

CONTENTS

A NOTE UPON THE POEMS   PAGE 7

TEXT   19

PLATES

Mirth and Her Companions   FRONTISPIECE

Night Startled by the Lark   23

The Great Sun   27

The Sunshine Holiday   31

The Stories of Corydon and Thyrsis   35

The Young Poet's Dream   39

A NOTE UPON THE POEMS

THE genesis of *L'Allegro* and *Il Penseroso*, perhaps the best known and most heartily admired of all Milton's compositions, is involved in considerable obscurity. They were not printed before 1645, and they do not exist for us in the celebrated bound volume of Milton's Mss. in the library of Trinity College, Cambridge, which contains the drafts of all the English poems written between 1633, probably, and 1645; we are therefore compelled, in the absence of other data, to rely upon inferences and internal evidence in determining their time and place of writing. The consensus of critical opinion gives 1631-34 as the time, and Horton as the place. Professor Masson assigns them to the latter half of 1632. There are, however, reasons to make one think that they should probably be placed earlier. The autumn of 1632 seems to be selected because Horton is usually assumed as the place of composition, and Milton went to reside there in July, 1632. He would naturally, argue the critics, be so impressed with the charms of the spot that he would turn to verse, and *L'Allegro* and *Il Penseroso*, and the *Song on May Morning*, which we have assigned to the Cambridge period, would be the outcome. But there is no proof that the poems were not written at Cambridge or in London as reminiscential tributes to the pleasures of a vacation spent in the country; and we know from a Latin prolusion or oration delivered, Masson thinks, either in the latter half of 1631 or the first part of 1632, that Milton spent "the last past summer . . . amid rural scenes and sequestered glades," and that he recalled "the supreme delight *he* had with the Muses." This vacation of 1631 may have been spent at Horton, for there is no proof that the elder Milton had not then acquired that property, and the young poet may have written his poems under the elms that so fascinated him, or have composed them on his return to college.

I incline to the former supposition. As we shall see, he was unquestionably supplied with hints for both his poems by Burton's *Anatomy*, surely a likely book for such a student as Milton to take with him on a vacation. Again, no one can read the *Prolusion on Earling Rising*, almost certainly Milton's, without thinking that much of the raw material of the two poems was in his brain and being expressed during his university life; nor can one read the other prolusions without seeing that Orpheus, the music of the spheres, and Platonism were much in his thoughts. Besides, about 1630, the date of the *Epitaph on Shakspere*, Milton was evidently to some extent occupied with his great forerunner, whose genius is honored in the poems, and a year later he was experimenting with the

8

octosyllabic couplet in the *Epitaph on the Marchioness of Winchester*. Finally, it was about this time that he was seriously weighing the reasons *pro* and *con* with regard to his choice of a profession, and it might naturally occur to him to contrast in poetic form the pleasures of the more or less worldly and the more or less secluded, studious, and devoted life. He had made his choice by the autumn of 1632, and had therefore less cause for such poetical expression.

A minute analysis of the style and metre of the poems tends to confirm the view expressed above. It is obviously a transitional style when compared with that of the *Nativity Ode*, and other earlier pieces. Scriptural ideas and subjects are occupying his mind less and he has progressed toward a freer handling of his themes. He has become interested in contemporary English poetry, and while showing the influence of the classics, is not mastered by them. All this would indicate that the poems were written after 1631, though, as we have just seen, it is not unlikely that having in that year handled the octosyllabic couplet successfully, he should shortly be tempted to try it again. We thus have 1631 as a *terminus a quo*; 1633-1634, the years of *Arcades* and *Comus*, are a *terminus ad quem* for the following strictly metrical reasons. The lyrical portions of *Arcades* and *Comus* appear to be less spontaneous and more mature than *L'Allegro* and its companion poem. The metrical art displayed is more elaborate and self-conscious, and when one looks closer, as, for example, when one compares the invocation to Mirth in *L'Allegro* with the similar passage in *Comus* (ll. 102-122), one is struck with the fact that the verses of the anti-masque have lost the blithe sensuousness of the former poem, that thought is struggling with feeling, and that the lyric style of the poet is approaching its culmination in the elaborate and highly sustained art that has made *Lycidas* matchless. We conclude, therefore, that *L'Allegro* and *Il Penseroso* are nearer to the *Epitaph on the Marchioness of Winchester* than they are to *Arcades;* and if any one should argue that the mature sentiment of the poems and their vigorous expression indicate a later, not an earlier, date, it must suffice to reply that youth takes itself more seriously than age, and that there is no sentiment or thought in either poem that Milton might not well have had as a student at Cambridge.

It has been stated already that Milton was indebted for hints, if not for direct suggestion, to Burton's *Anatomy of Melancholy*. This famous book, the first edition of which appeared 1621, was prefaced by a poem entitled *The Author's Abstract of Melancholy*, Διαλογῶς, in which "Democritus Junior" analyzes his feelings in a way that foreshadows Milton's subsequent procedure. There are twelve stanzas of eight lines each, the last two verses of each stanza constituting a variable refrain, the measure being, however, the octosyllabic couplet. In one stanza the pleasures of a meditative man are given in a series of little pictures, while the next stanza presents the woes of the same personage when a fit of real melancholy is upon him. Milton could not have failed to be struck with the general effectiveness of the idea and its development, but his artist's instinct told him that this effectiveness would be enhanced if, instead of a dialogue in stanzas, he should write two distinct but companion poems, developed on parallel lines, in which the pleasures of a typically cheerful and a typically serious man should be described in pictures slightly more elaborate than those of Burton. He abandoned the too glaring contrast of joys and woes, and succeeded also in avoiding the occasional dropping into commonplace that mars the *Abstract of Melancholy*. But some pictures and even lines and phrases of the elder poem probably remained in his memory.

Another poem which may have influenced Milton is the song, "Hence, all you vain delights," in Fletcher's play, *The Nice Valour*. This play was not published until 1647, but it had been acted long before, and the song had almost certainly become known before *Il Penseroso* was written. Tradition assigns the lyric to Beaumont, but Mr. Bullen with more probability gives it to Fletcher. It is an exquisite expansion of the theme expressed in its closing verse, "Nothing's so dainty-sweet as lovely melancholy," and it is pleasant to believe that it may have given Milton a hint, although it can scarcely have had as much influence upon his verses as his own two poems plainly had upon a stanza of Collin's *The Passions*. There are naturally traces of other poets to be found in these productions of Milton's impressionable period, particularly of Joshua Sylvester, and to a less degree of Spenser, Browne, and Marlowe. Collins, too, was not the only eighteenth-century poet who had *L'Allegro* and *Il Penseroso* ringing through his head, as any one may see who will take the trouble to examine Dodsley's well-known collection. Even Pope was not above borrowing epithets from them, and Dyer's best poem, "Grongar Hill," would not have had its being without them. Matthew Green, Thomas Warton, John Hughes, who actually wrote a new conclusion for *Il Penseroso*, and other minor verse-writers were much affected by them, and Gray borrowed from them with the open boldness that always marks the appropriations of a true poet. But perhaps the best proof of their popularity during a century which is too sweepingly charged with inability to appreciate real poetry, is the fact that Handel set them to music. In our own century they have never lacked admirers, or failed to exert upon poets an easily detected influence. It may even be held with some show of reason that their popularity, leading to a fuller knowledge of Milton, paved the way for the remarkable renaissance of Spenser in the eighteenth and nineteenth centuries.

As their Italian titles imply, the subjects or speakers of Milton's verses are The Cheerful Man and The Thoughtful (Meditative) Man respectively. Our English adjectives do not quite adequately render the Italian they are intended to translate, which is perhaps the reason why Milton went abroad for his titles, since he had a striking warning before him in Burton's *Abstract* of the ambiguity attaching to such a word as "melancholy," which he might have used with one of his poems without exciting surprise. He has excited surprise with some modern critics through the fact that he wrote *Penseroso* instead of *Pensieroso*, but it has been seemingly shown that the form he used was correct and current when he wrote. His Italian titles, however, have not prevented much discussion as to the characters he intended to portray. Critics are quite unanimously of the opinion that *Il Penseroso* represents a man very like the Milton we know, but they are divided as to the kind of man typified by *L'Allegro*. One editor, Mr. Verity, goes so far as to

13

say that Milton "must have felt that the character of *L'Allegro* might, with slight changes or additions, be made to typify the careless, pleasure-seeking spirit of the Cavaliers and Court; the spirit which he afterward figured in Comus and his followers, and condemned to destruction." If this view be correct, one is forced to conclude that Milton had more of the true dramatist's power of creating characters other than himself than he has generally been supposed to possess; and it requires us to conceive the more sprightly poem as forming a hard mechanical contrast to its companion, which is the reverse of poetical. On the other hand, Dr. Garnett maintains that the two poems "are complementary rather than contrary, and may be, in a sense, regarded as one poem, whose theme is the praise of the reasonable life." It is easy to agree with this view, especially as Burton's poem obviously suggested the idea of contrasting two well-marked moods of one individual character, rather than that of bringing into juxtaposition two radically different characters. *L'Allegro* may not be the Milton who meditated entering the Church and making his life a true poem, but he is rather the Milton who went to the theatre in his youth than the typical Cavalier of Charles's court. Cavaliers did not usually call for "sweet Liberty" but for sweet License, nor did they greatly hanker after "unreproved

14

pleasures." They were not particularly noted for their early rising; and if any one of them had watched the Bear out, in different pursuits from those of *Il Penseroso*, he would probably not have continued his morning walk after encountering the "milkmaid singing blithe."

Another point on which critics differ is, whether or not Milton intended to describe the events of a day of twenty-four hours. Some claim that he merely sketches the general tenor of the life of his characters; others that he represents the events of an ideal day. The antagonists ought to be satisfied with the assurance that he intended to do both the one thing and the other. The careful and sequential division of the day that is apparent in each poem (even if *Il Penseroso* does begin with the nightingale and the moon) cannot be accidental, nor can the grouping of events and natural sights belonging to different seasons of the year be the result of ignorance.

It is, probably, a fad of criticism to call as much attention as is now done to the fact that Milton was not so accurate or so penetrating an observer of nature as some of his successors, like Tennyson, have been. In the first place, neither here nor in *Paradise Lost* will Milton be found to be much of a sinner in this regard if he be compared with his predecessors and contemporaries. In the second place, it is by no means certain that

15

minute and accurate observation of nature is essential to the equipment of a great poet. A genuine love of nature, a power to feel and impart something of her spirit, is doubtless essential; but as poetry on its pictorial side should be mainly suggestive, it is not yet clear that posterity will get more pleasure out of the elaborate and accurate pictures of some modern poets than out of the broadly true and suggestive, if sometimes inaccurate, pictures of Milton. It is not entirely unlikely that our recently developed love of detail-work has injured our sense for form, and that our grandchildren will take Matthew Arnold's advice and return to the Greeks—and Milton, in order to learn what the highest poetry really is like. Milton is nearer akin to Homer and Sophocles than he is to the modern naturalist or nature mystic, and it is well for English poetry that he is. He would probably have thought the picture of the sunbeams lying in the golden chamber, suggested by a few words in that exquisite fragment of Mimnermus beginning "Αζηταω πόλιν," more in keeping with the requirements of a rational poetics than nine-tenths of the purple descriptive passages in English poetry since the days of Wordsworth.

Yet if editors and critics have had their humors and fads, they have always ended by acknowledging the perennial charm of these poems. And the mass of readers has paid its highest tribute of culling many a phrase and verse for quotation.

L' ALLEGRO

BY

JOHN MILTON
&
WILLIAM BLAKE

L'ALLEGRO

Hence loathèd Melancholy,

   Of Cerberus and blackest Midnight born,

In Stygian Cave forlorn

   'Mongst horrid shapes, and shrieks, and sights unholy!

Find out some uncouth cell,

   Where brooding Darkness spreads his jealous wings,

And the night-Raven sings;

   There under Ebon shades, and low-browed Rocks,

As ragged as thy Locks,

   In dark Cimmerian desert ever dwell.

But come, thou Goddess fair and free,

In Heaven yclept Euphrosyne,

And by men, heart-easing Mirth,

Whom lovely Venus, at a birth,

With two sister Graces more,

To Ivy-crownèd Bacchus bore;

Or whether (as some Sager sing)

The Frolic Wind that breathes the Spring,

Zephir with Aurora playing,

As he met her once a-Maying,

There, on Beds of Violets blue,

And fresh-blown Roses washed in dew,

Filled her with thee, a daughter fair,

So buxom, blithe, and debonair.

　　Haste thee, Nymph, and bring with thee

Jest and youthful Jollity,

Quips and Cranks, and wanton Wiles,

Nods, and Becks, and Wreathèd Smiles,

Such as hang on Hebe's cheek,

And love to live in dimple sleek;

Sport that wrinkled Care derides,

And Laughter holding both his sides.

Come, and trip it as ye go

On the light fantastic toe,

And in thy right hand lead with thee,

The Mountain Nymph, sweet Liberty;

And if I give thee honor due,

Mirth, admit me of thy crew

To live with her, and live with thee,

In unreprovèd pleasures free;

To hear the Lark begin his flight,

And, singing, startle the dull night,

From his watch-tower in the skies,

Till the dappled dawn doth rise;

Then to come in spite of sorrow,

And at my window bid good-morrow,

Through the Sweet-Briar, or the Vine,

Or the twisted Eglantine.

While the Cock, with lively din,

NIGHT STARTLED BY THE LARK

Scatters the rear of darkness thin,

And to the stack, or the Barn-door,

Stoutly struts his Dames before,

Oft listening how the Hounds and horn

Clearly rouse the slumbering morn,

From the side of some Hoar Hill,

Through the high wood echoing shrill.

Some time walking not unseen

By Hedge-row Elms, on Hillocks green,

Right against the Eastern gate,

Where the great Sun begins his state,

Robed in flames, and Amber light,

The clouds in thousand Liveries dight.

While the Plowman, near at hand,

Whistles o'er the Furrowed Land,

And the Milkmaid singeth blithe,

And the Mower whets his scythe,

And every Shepherd tells his tale

Under the Hawthorn in the dale.

Straight mine eye hath caught new pleasures

Whilst the Landscape round it measures,

Russet Lawns, and Fallows Gray,

Where the nibbling flocks do stray,

Mountains on whose barren breast

The laboring clouds do often rest:

Meadows trim with Daisies pied,

THE GREAT SUN

Shallow Brooks, and Rivers wide.

Towers, and Battlements it sees

Bosomed high in tufted Trees,

Where perhaps some beauty lies,

The Cynosure of neighboring eyes.

Hard by a Cottage chimney smokes,

From betwixt two aged Oaks,

Where Corydon and Thyrsis met,

Are at their savory dinner set

Of Herbs, and other Country Messes,

Which the neat-handed Phillis dresses;

And then in haste her Bower she leaves,

With Thestylis to bind the Sheaves;

Or, if the earlier season lead,

To the tanned Haycock in the Mead.

Sometimes with secure delight

The upland Hamlets will invite,

When the merry Bells ring round,

And the jocund rebecks sound

To many a youth, and many a maid,

Dancing in the Chequered shade;

And young and old come forth to play

On a Sunshine Holyday,

Till the live-long day-light fail;

Then to the Spicy Nut-brown Ale,

With stories told of many a feat,

THE SUNSHINE HOLIDAY

How Faery Mab the junkets eat.

She was pinched, and pulled she said;

And he, by Friar's Lantern led,

Tells how the drudging Goblin sweat,

To earn his Cream-bowl duly set,

When in one night, ere glimpse of morn,

His shadowy Flail hath threshed the Corn

That ten day-laborers could not end,

Then lies him down, the lubber fiend,

And stretched out all the Chimney's length,

Basks at the fire his hairy strength;

And Crop-full out of doors he flings,

Ere the first Cock his Matin rings.

Thus done the Tales, to bed they creep,

By whispering Winds soon lulled asleep.

Towered Cities please us then,

And the busy hum of men,

Where throngs of Knights and Barons bold,

In weeds of Peace high triumphs hold,

With store of Ladies, whose bright eyes

Rain influence, and judge the prize

Of Wit, or Arms, while both contend

To win her Grace, whom all commend.

There let Hymen oft appear

In Saffron robe, with Taper clear,

And pomp, and feast, and revelry,

THE STORIES OF CORYDON AND THYRSIS

With mask, and antique Pageantry,

Such sights as youthful Poets dream

On Summer eves by haunted stream.

Then to the well-trod stage anon,

If Jonson's learnèd Sock be on,

Or sweetest Shakespeare, Fancy's child,

Warble his native Wood-notes wild;

And ever, against eating Cares,

Lap me in soft Lydian Airs,

Married to immortal verse

Such as the meeting soul may pierce

In notes, with many a winding bout

Of linkèd sweetness long drawn out,

With wanton heed, and giddy cunning,

The melting voice through mazes running;

Untwisting all the chains that tie

The hidden soul of harmony;

That Orpheus' self may heave his head

From golden slumber on a bed

Of heaped Elysian flowers, and hear

Such strains as would have won the ear

Of Pluto, to have quite set free

His half-regained Eurydice.

These delights, if thou canst give,

Mirth, with thee I mean to live.

THE YOUNG POET'S DREAM

BLAKE'S INSCRIPTIONS ON HIS PAINTINGS

MIRTH AND HER COMPANIONS

These personifications are all brought together in the First design Surrounding the Principal Figure which is Mirth herself.

NIGHT STARTLED BY THE LARK

The Lark is an Angel on the Wing. Dull Night starts from his Watch Tower on a Cloud. The Dawn with her Dappled Horses arises above the Earth. The Earth beneath awakes at the Lark's Voice.

THE GREAT SUN

The Great Sun is represented clothed in Flames, Surrounded by the Clouds in their Liveries, in their various Offices at the Eastern Gate; beneath, in Small Figures, Milton walking by Elms on Hillocks green, The Plowman, The Milkmaid, The Mower whetting his Scythe, and The Shepherd and his Lass under a Hawthorn in the Dale.

THE SUNSHINE HOLIDAY

In this design is Introduced,

Mountains on whose barren breast
The labouring clouds do often rest.

Mountains, Clouds, Rivers, Trees appear Humanized on the Sunshine Holiday. The Church Steeple with its merry bells. The Clouds arise from the bosoms of Mountains, While Two Angels sound their Trumpets in the Heavens to announce the Sunshine Holiday.

THE STORIES OF CORYDON AND THYRSIS

The Goblin crop full flings out of doors from his Laborious task dropping his Flail & Cream bowl, yawning & stretching, vanishes into the Sky, in which is seen Queen Mab Eating the Junkets. The Sports of the Fairies are seen thro' the Cottage where "She" lays in Bed, 'pinch'd & pull'd' by Fairies as they dance on the Bed, the Ceiling & the Floor, & a Ghost pulls the Bed Clothes at her Feet. "He" is seen following the Friar's Lantern towards the Convent.

THE YOUNG POET'S DREAM

The Youthful Poet, sleeping on a bank by the Haunted Stream by Sun Set, sees in his dream the more bright Sun of Imagination under the auspices of Shakespeare & Johnson [Jonson], in which is Hymen at a Marriage & the Antique Pageantry attending it.

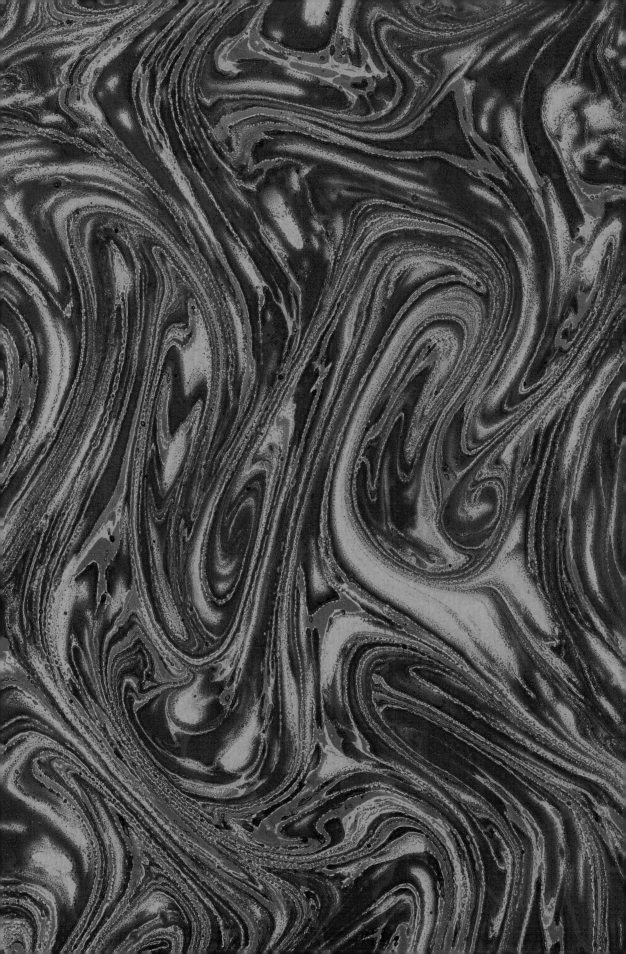